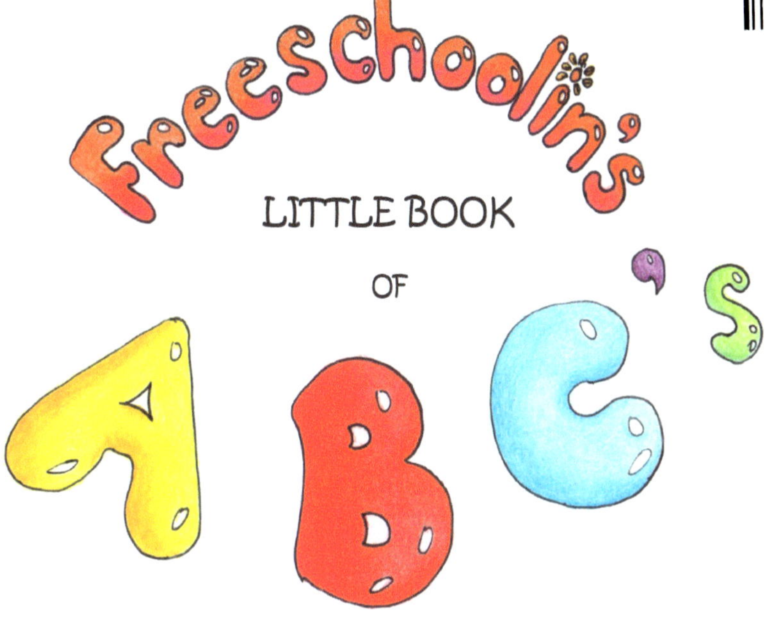

Dedicated to the amazing Unschoolers who teach themselves to read, and the Parents who facilitate them.

Freeschoolin's Little Book of ABC's
Text and Illustrations copyright © Wendy Elizabeth Hart

Editing by Jaze Hart.

First Edition

ISBN 978-0-9959219-6-2(pbk.)

Published By Hart2Hart Art Publishing

HART2HART ART

PUBLISHING

Freeschoolin's

LITTLE BOOK

OF

ABC's

featuring the Roundies!

apple

A

acorn

is for

axolotl

bumble bee

B

beach ball

is for

bird

crab

C

candy

is for

COW

doughnut

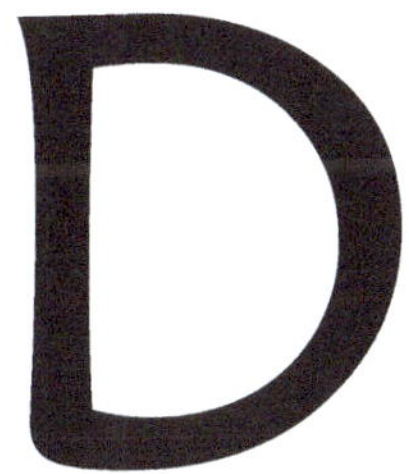

D

duck

is for

dog

earthworm

E

egg

is for

elephant

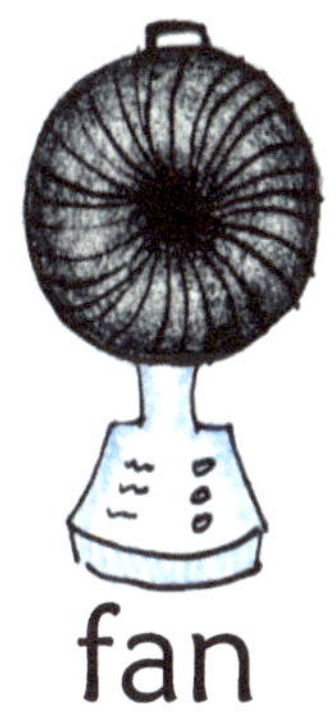

fan

F

flower

is for

fish

goat

grapes

is for

grizzly bear

hive

H

honey

is for

horse

icicles

I

ice cream

is for

iguana

jam

J

jackrabbit

is for

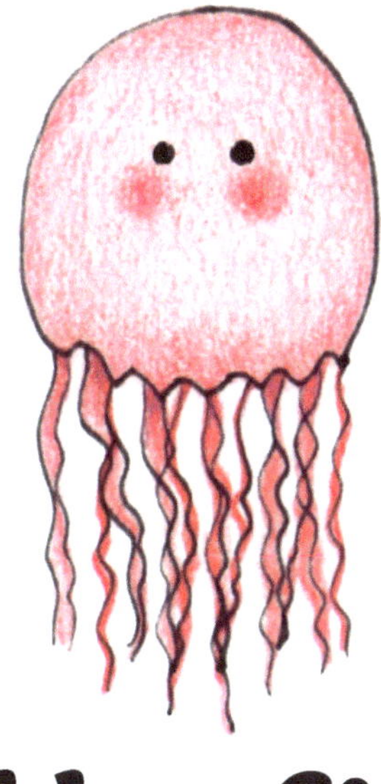

jellyfish

knife

K

kite

is for

kitten

lollipop

L

lion

is for

ladybug

moon

M

muffin

is for

monkey

is for

narwhal

orange

O

olives

is for

octopus

P

is for

python

quill

Q

quilt

is for

quail

ribbon

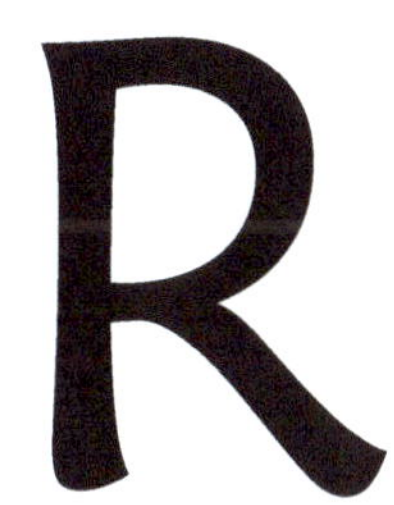

R

rubber boots

is for

rhinoceros

is for

sheep

tennis racket

T

turtle

is for

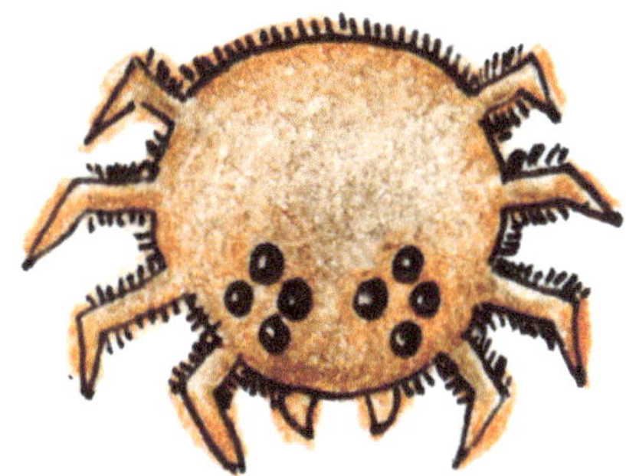

tarantula

umbrella

U

unicycle

is for

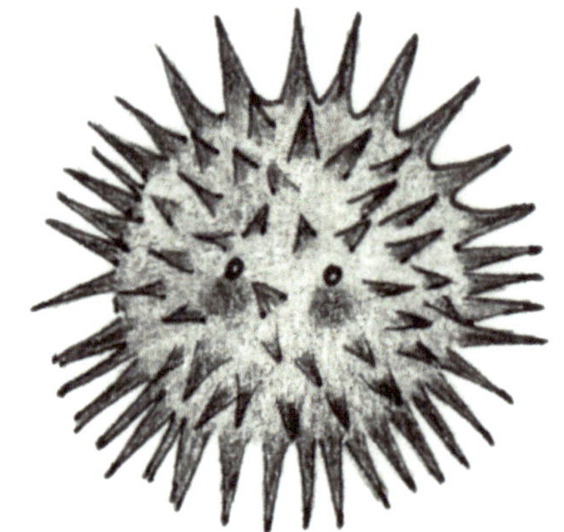

urchin

vegetables

V

vase

is for

vampire bat

whale

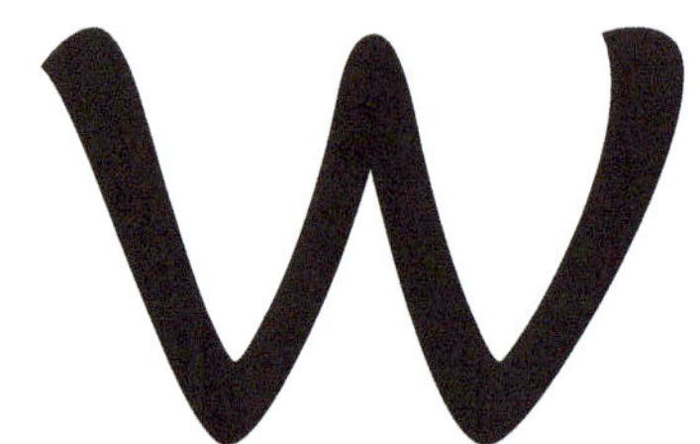

wolf

is for

wombat

xylophone

X

xyris

is for

xantus's
hummingbird

yo-yo

Y

yarn

is for

yak

zucchini

Z

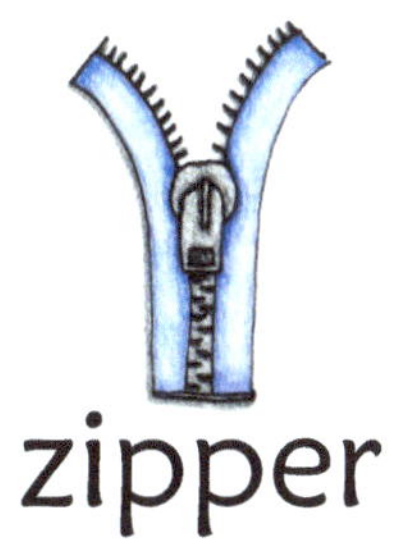

zipper

is for

zebra

featuring the Roundies!

About the Author

Wendy Elizabeth Hart

"Thank you for being a part of our Freeschoolin' journey.
Much Love Always. " -Wendy Elizabeth Hart

Wendy Elizabeth Hart is a grateful Mom of two, and a talented professional artist,
married to her best friend, living an unschooled, homesteading life.
Through observing her daughter and other unschoolers teach themselves, Wendy was inspired to
create the Freeschoolin's Little Book of ABC's.

About the Editor/Publisher
Jaze Hart

Jaze is a happily married, doting unschool Dad and has edited and published all of the
Freeschoolin' Books available.

You can follow Wendy and her family on social media linked on the Freeschoolin' website, as well
as past blog posts, the Freeschoolin' bookstore and free resources like colouring pages, journal
templates and more.

https://horsewhisperer333.wixsite.com/freeschoolin